Dedication
To my dear Dad,
Thanks for believing and encouraging me to never stop being creative!

*Happy Reading
Best wishes,*

*Tsi. McLure
3/18/2022*

For their science project Lily, Ryan and Mia got together to find out what Infection Preventionist known as Germ Fighting Heroes do. They were so surprised to find out that the Germ fighters (Infection Preventionists) wears many hats of responsibilities.

Lily: Mia please let Ryan know that we can meet at the Gym to put our project together.
Mia: Ok, will do.

Ryan: Can I tell you about what I found out first?
Lily & Mia: Yeah, go ahead.

Ryan: An Infection Preventionist is a healthcare provider like a nurse or medical technologist or an epidemiologist who receive extra training in the field of Microbiology. Microbiology is the study of microorganisms such as viruses, bacteria.

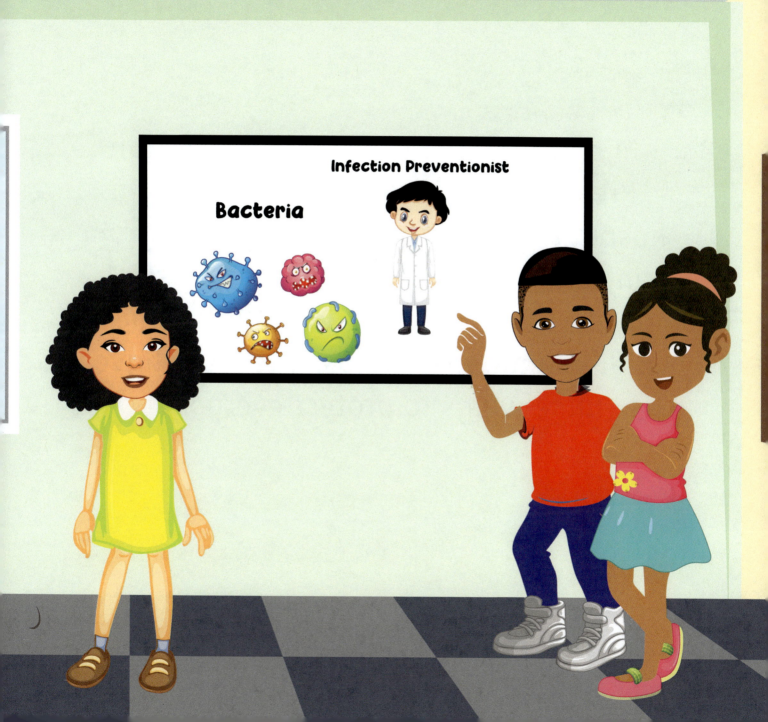

Mia: One of the duties of an Infection Preventionist is to protect patients in hospital and protect all the workers from infections caused by microorganisms. It's like a mother hen, with all the chicks hiding under her wings. She must have huge wings to protect everyone!

Lily: Mia, I like your imagination but let's talk about how an Infection Preventionist hunts for these infections in order to protect everyone. Does she use a microscope to check for viruses and bacteria?

Mia: No, she works with lots of other trained people such as, epidemiologist & microbiologist, who will use a microscope to check for viruses and bacteria that cause infection.

Ryan: An Infection Preventionist also educates everyone on good hand hygiene because good hand hygiene is the number 1 defense against microorganism.

Mia: Ryan where did you find that information?

Ryan: I found it on the CDC website

Ryan: I also found out that Infection Preventionist work hand-in-hand with Physicians as they treat patients and writes orders for antibiotics.
Infection Preventionist is able to see if the person has been given too many antibiotics.
Mia: I read about it too. Antibiotics should not be taken like candy! You need to allow your body to fight some of the infection by itself.

Lily: I found out that an Infection Preventionist is a person who works with everyone throughout the hospital. Infection Preventionist gives advice on proper hand washing; wearing personal, protective equipment (PPE) to stop the spread of germs.

Ryan: Infection Preventionist monitors Kitchen staff as they prepare food for patients and staff. The food should be cooked and stored well to stop the spread of germs.

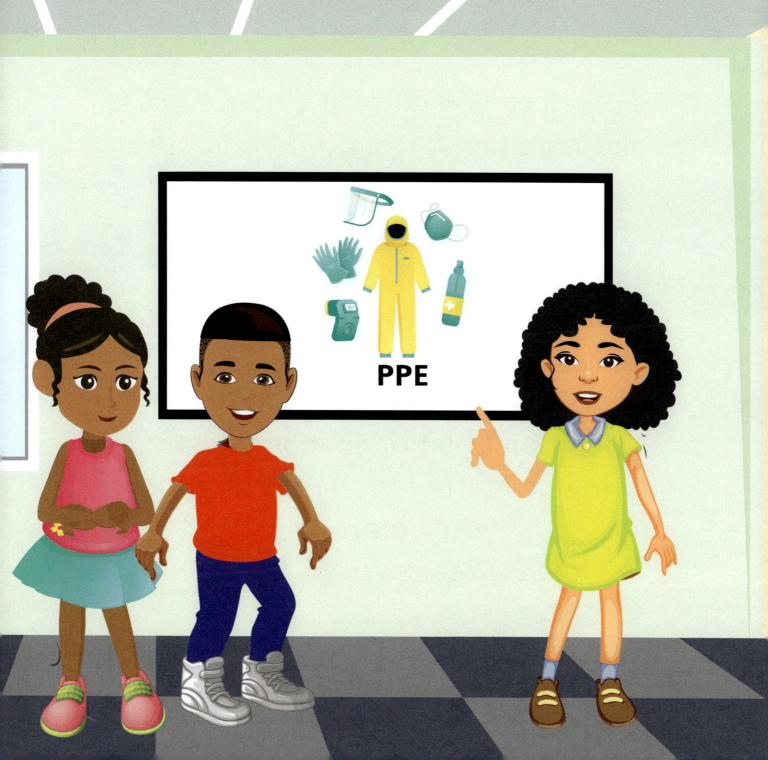

Mia: Have you all seen a notice in the bathroom of a restaurant and other places we buy food?

Ryan: What notice Mia?

Mia: It says, employees please wash your hands before going back to work.

Lily & Ryan: Oh yeah, we have seen that notice.

Mia: Don't you think it should read: everyone must wash hands after using the bathroom?

Ryan: That's such a neat idea!

Mia: An Infection Preventionist also monitors Housekeeping staff as they move from room-to-room cleaning and changing linen. They have to be careful to stop the spread of germs!

Lily: I was surprised to read that they work with Hospital engineers too!

Mia: Really, work with engineers, why?

Lily: To help monitor all the building work done in the hospital because sick patients should not get dust in their rooms. Engineers also check the showers, drinking water or ice cubes in order to stop the spread of germs!

Mia: That's so interesting. When my grandma was in hospital, my parents were not allowed to bring fresh plants and some fresh fruit.

Lily: Was it because fresh fruit will bring fruit flies?

Mia: That one too! The nurse said that my grandma was not allowed to eat the fruit and the soil on the fresh plants may have germs that would make her sick.

I love my grandma; she is fine now.

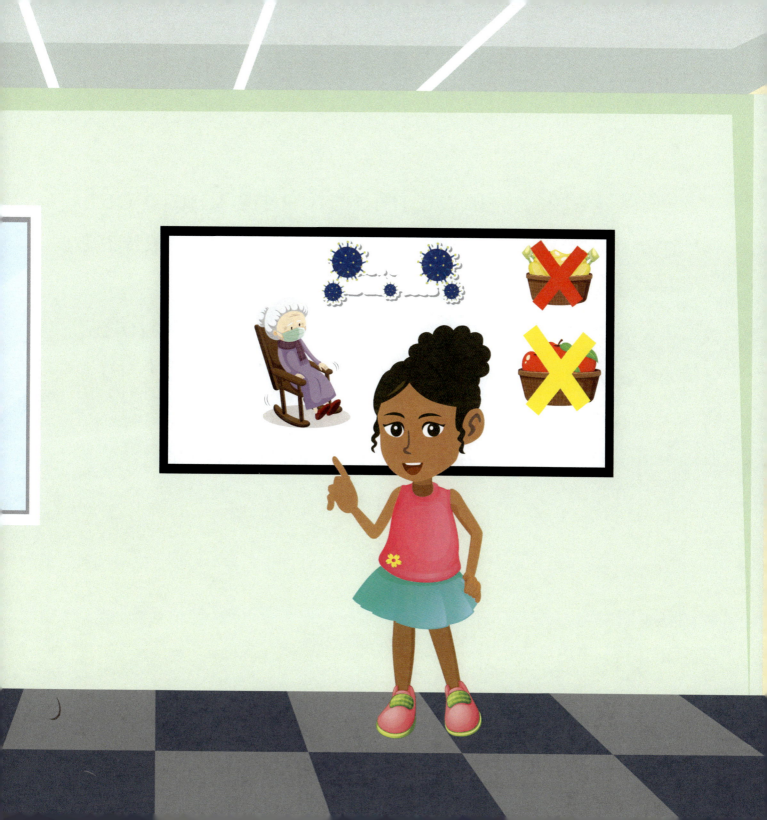

Mia: Let's hear from Ryan if he found out even more of what Infection Preventionist does.

Ryan: I also found out that an Infection Preventionist teaches all staff about flu shots and other shots needed for their protection and to stop the spread of germs!

Ryan: I almost forgot that an Infection Preventionist also tracks all infections and checks carefully to see if the infections are going up or down. Then gives a report to the hospital leaders to keep them up to date.

Lily: I found out how an Infection Preventionist also lets the State know quickly about anyone who has a disease that can spread to others, such as TB or measles or a dreadful virus such as Covid, so that the State staff can investigate further to stop the spread of disease to others in the community.

Mia: Some Infection Preventionists work in the community like nursing homes to monitor and prevent the spread of germs!

Lily: Also encouraging staff not to come to work if they are sick to stop the spread of germs!

Mia: This was the best project we did together!

Mia: We have made a long list of work that Infection Preventionists do. That is why they are called Germ Fighting Heroes.

Ryan: I agree, Infection Preventionists are awesome heroes.

Lily: They are definitely heroes for working with other heroes to keep us all safe!

Made in the USA
Middletown, DE
08 January 2022